Engineers
Solve
Problems

Reagan Miller
& Crystal Sikkens

Crabtree Publishing Company
www.crabtreebooks.com

Authors
Reagan Miller
Crystal Sikkens

Publishing plan research and development:
Reagan Miller

Editor
Kathy Middleton

Design
Samara Parent

Photo research
Reagan Miller
Samara Parent
Crystal Sikkens

**Production coordinator
and prepress technician**
Samara Parent

Print coordinator
Margaret Amy Salter

Photographs
© Juice Images/Alamy: page 19
Dreamstime: page 5 (bottom-plane)
Fotolia: page 5 (bottom-except plane)
iStockphoto: pages 13 (bottom left), 21
Thinkstock: cover (left), page 8 (top right)
All other images by Shutterstock

Library and Archives Canada Cataloguing in Publication

Miller, Reagan, author
        Engineers solve problems / Reagan Miller and Crystal Sikkens.

(Engineering close-up)
Includes index.
Issued in print and electronic formats.
ISBN 978-0-7787-0094-4 (bound).--ISBN 978-0-7787-0101-9 (pbk.).--
ISBN 978-1-4271-9405-3 (pdf).--ISBN 978-1-4271-9401-5 (html)

        1. Engineers--Juvenile literature. 2. Problem solving--Juvenile
literature. I. Sikkens, Crystal, author II. Title.

TA157.M557 2013   j620   C2013-906288-2
                                          C2013-906289-0

Library of Congress Cataloging-in-Publication Data

CIP available at Library of Congress

Crabtree Publishing Company

www.crabtreebooks.com   1-800-387-7650

Printed in Canada/032014/MA20140124

Published in Canada
Crabtree Publishing
616 Welland Ave.
St. Catharines, Ontario
L2M 5V6

Published in the United States
Crabtree Publishing
PMB 59051
350 Fifth Avenue, 59th Floor
New York, New York 10118

Published in the United Kingdom
Crabtree Publishing
Maritime House
Basin Road North, Hove
BN41 1WR

Published in Australia
Crabtree Publishing
3 Charles Street
Coburg North
VIC 3058

Contents

Solving problems

Imagine you are in the library. A book you really want to read is on the top shelf and you cannot reach it. What do you do?

a) Wait until you grow taller.

b) Wait by the shelf and hope that an adult comes by to help.

c) Make a plan to create something to solve your problem so you can safely reach your book.

Who are engineers?

If you chose "c," you are already thinking like an **engineer**! Engineers are people who use math, science, and creative thinking to **design** things to solve problems. To design is to make a plan for how something is made or built.

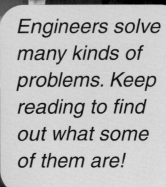

Engineers solve many kinds of problems. Keep reading to find out what some of them are!

Plenty of problems

What do you think when you hear the word "problem"? Many people think a problem is something bad. Engineers, however, are people who enjoy solving problems—in fact, engineers are professional problem solvers!

An engineer might design a bridge so cars and trucks can cross a river.

Super solvers!

There are many different kinds of problems, so different kinds of engineers are needed to solve them. Things that allow us to **communicate** with people far away, travel quickly from place to place, and stay warm in cold weather were all designed by different kinds of engineers.

What things are keeping these people warm on this snowy day?

This girl is communicating over the phone with a friend far away.

What do engineers design?

The things engineers design are called **technologies**. A technology is anything made by a person to solve a problem or meet a need. For example, what do you do if your pencil breaks while you are writing? You use a pencil sharpener. A pencil sharpener is a technology that solves your broken pencil problem!

A pencil sharpener quickly sharpens your pencil so you can keep writing.

fan

light bulb

What do you think?

Look at the pictures below. Each photograph shows a technology. What problem does each technology solve?

alarm clock

umbrella

Tool technologies

Long ago, people solved problems using simple technologies such as **tools**. Tools are objects that people use to make work easier and faster. Different tools are made for different kinds of work. Tools help people meet their needs.

All people need shelter. Tools such as hammers, drills, and saws can be used to build shelters, like this house.

Tool-time travel

Many of our needs today are the same as they were long ago. Some of the same tools designed long ago are still being used today. However, some work better now than they did before. This is because engineers not only create new technologies, they also **improve** them, or make the ones we have better.

What do you think?

Can you match up the tools from long ago and today? Can you tell how the tools have improved?

11

The design process

The Engineering Design Process is a set of steps that engineers use as a guide to help them solve problems. The Engineering Design Process helps engineers find the best **solution**, or answer, to a problem.

1. Find a problem
Ask questions about the problem to learn about it.

5. Communicate
Share your design with others.

2. Brainstorm solutions

Work with a group to come up with different ways to solve the problem.

Solution

3. Plan and make a model

As a group, choose the best solution. Create a plan to make a model of the solution. Gather materials and make your model.

4. Test and improve

Test your model. Record the results. Use the test results to help make your design better. Retest your improved design.

13

What's the problem?

The first step in the Engineering Design Process is finding a problem to solve. Engineers look for problems to solve that can help others, improve something that isn't working, or help the environment.

An engineer might look for a way to make something easier for elderly or disabled people to do.

Find out more

Before they start solving a problem, engineers must first make sure the problem hasn't already been solved before. Then they need to gather information to better understand why the problem needs to be solved.

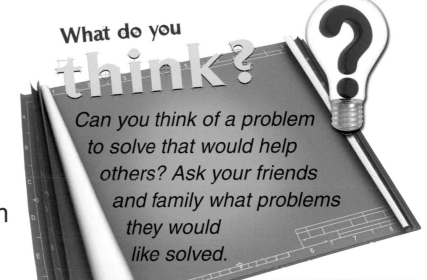

What do you think?

Can you think of a problem to solve that would help others? Ask your friends and family what problems they would like solved.

Talking to others, asking questions, and doing research are helpful ways to gather information.

15

Super solutions!

Once engineers understand the problem, they think about possible solutions. There are often many different solutions to a problem. Engineers look for the solution that best meets the needs of the problem.

Engineers often work with others to find the best solution to a problem.

Brilliant brainstorming!

Brainstorming is a group activity used to share ideas. Engineers use brainstorming to create a list of possible solutions. When brainstorming, only one person speaks at a time while everyone else listens. Everyone has a chance to speak, and no one judges another person's ideas. All ideas are written down.

What do you think?

Work with some friends and brainstorm other possible solutions to fill in the empty circles below.

put wheels on the bottom of backpacks so we can pull them

photocopy only the pages you need to complete the homework

Problem statement: Our backpacks are too heavy to carry home at the end of the day.

put motors inside backpacks so we can drive them home

17

Making models

Engineers decide as a group which solution is the best to solve the problem. To help explain their idea and find out whether their solution will work, engineers often build **models**. A model is a **representation** of a real object. It can show how something will look or how different parts of an object work together.

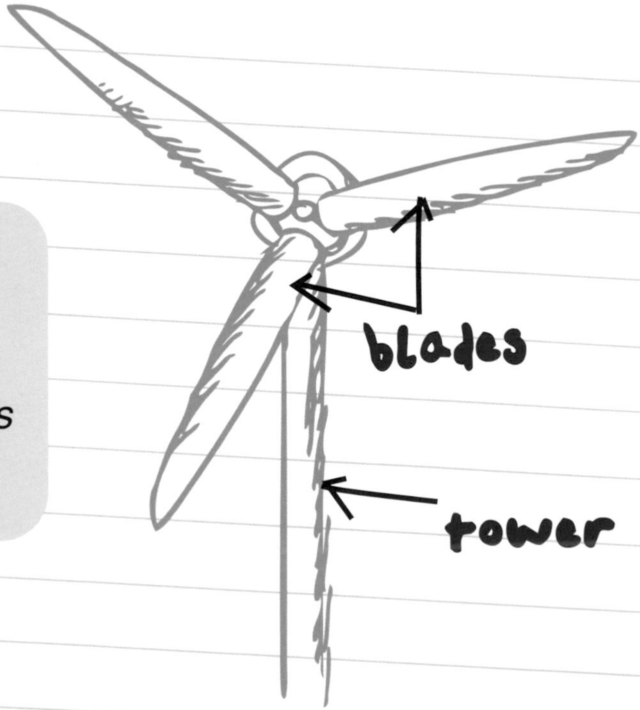

*A model can be a solid object, a drawing, or a **diagram**. This diagram shows the different parts of a **wind turbine**.*

blades

tower

Testing models

A model may not have all the same parts or details as the real object, but a model can help people understand the engineer's idea for solving the problem. Testing a model is a good way to see whether an idea will work. It can also tell an engineer what things need to be fixed or changed.

*This child is testing his model wind turbine to see whether it can produce enough electricity to power a house. Wind energy helps the environment because it does not create **pollution**.*

Problem-solving kids

Anyone can become an engineer! Kids just like you have designed technologies that solve problems. Cassidy Goldstein was 11 years old when she designed a holder for broken crayons. At age nine, Chris Haas designed a basketball with handprints on it to show kids where to put their hands when shooting a basket.

Excellent earmuffs

Did you know March 13 is Earmuff Day in the United States? Thanks to 15-year-old Chester Greenwood's invention in 1873, earmuffs have become one of the best ways to keep our ears warm on a cold day.

Chester wanted to find a way to keep his ears warm while ice skating. He designed earmuffs to solve his problem. He solved this problem for others too!

Be a problem solver

The world is full of problems waiting to be solved—
you just have to find them! Think of a problem
to solve that would help people, animals,
or the environment. Follow the steps of
the Engineering Design Process to help
you find a solution
to your problem.

Here's some problems to get you started:
-Design a tool to peel an orange without
getting sticky hands.
-Find a safe way to pick up garbage to help
keep the environment clean.
-Design something to help keep your dog
dry when it goes out in the rain.

Learning more

Books

Rocks, Jeans, and Busy Machines: An Engineering Kids Storybook by Alane and Raymundo Rivera. Rivera Engineering, 2010.

Rosie Revere, Engineer, by Andrea Beaty. Henry N. Abrams Publishing, 2013.

Thomas Edison for Kids: His Life and Ideas, by Laurie Carlson. Chicago Review Press, 2006.

Websites

This website provides videos showing kids engaged in design challenges. There are also several engineering challenges for kids to try!
http://pbskids.org/designsquad

This Science NetLinks' website challenges children to ask questions, explore solutions, and work together to solve challenges.
http://sciencenetlinks.com/tools/invention-at-play/

This website offers creative engineering challenges and the latest engineering news for kids.
http://www.inventivekids.com

Words to know

Note: Some bolded words are defined in the text

communicate (Kuh-MYOO-ni-keyt) *verb* To share thoughts and feelings in a way that makes them clearly understood

diagram (DAHY-uh-gram) noun A drawing or plan that helps explain something

engineer (en-juh-NIHR) noun A person who uses math, science, and creative thinking to design things that solve problems and meet needs

pollution (puh-LOO-shuhn) noun Waste that can harm land, water, and air

representation (rep-ri-zen-TA-shuhn) noun Something that stands in place of another thing with similar features

wind turbine (wind TUR-bin) noun A windmill that changes wind energy into electricity

A noun is a person, place, or thing. A verb is an action word that tells you what someone or something does.

Index